Indian Dolls

Nancy N. Schiffer

Schiffer Publishing Ltd

4880 Lower Valley Road, Atglen, PA 19310

ISBN: 0-7643-0305-8

Printed in China

Book Design by Blair R.C. Loughrey

Published by Schiffer Publishing Ltd.
77 Lower Valley Road
Atglen, PA 19310
Phone: (610) 593-1777; Fax: (610) 593-2002
E-mail: schifferbk@aol.com
Please write for a free catalog.
This book may be purchased from the publisher.
Please include $2.95 for shipping.
Try your bookstore first.

We are interested in hearing from authors
with book ideas on related subjects.

☼ Contents ☼

☼ *Acknowledgements* ☼

Lynn D. Trusdell, at Crown & Eagle Antiques in New Hope, Pennsylvania, showed me some of her treasured American Indian beadwork and collection of dolls one day, and I was captivated by the fine craftsmanship they possess. I could see that they were as diverse as the cultures that inspired them, and asked questions that seemed elementary, but expressed my vast ignorance of their backgrounds. Lynn is patient and polite. On another visit she had a few more to share with me, and finally said there ought to be a book written about the dolls; I suspect she knew of one or two others who were as fascinated as I was. Time went by. Lynn reiterated her idea. Eventually, Jeff Snyder took pictures of many of Lynn's dolls, and the book was underway. Lynn and her daughter Robin Mays found many treasured dolls for this study. Gale and Pat Kline at Kline's Galleries in Boonesboro, Maryland, learned of the project and offered to share some of their dolls, for they had also gathered some for their personal enjoyment. Martha Lawrence of Beaufort, South Carolina provided background photographs of the Southeast coastal region for the Seminole section. The party was growing. Later, Patty Fawn of the Lelooska Gallery in Ariel, Washington, told Vicki Yeske of Lebanon, Oregon, about the project and Vicki shared her enthusiasm for the Skookum dolls. Karen Norris found more valuable information and passed it along. Linda Edward of The Doll Museum in Newport, Rhode Island, located wonderful dolls to offer. Jack Bryan and Heddy Mann of Alaska on Madison in New York City drew from their shop and personal collections of Alaskan and Inuit dolls and contributed pictures for the book.

All of these charming dolls have touched so many people's lives already, and still the circle grows. I sincerely appreciate the help each of you has given me.

The photographs are courtesy of Lynn D. Trusdell unless otherwise noted.

☼ Preface ☼

The delightful and beautiful dolls in this book represent many different time periods, methods of construcion, regions of North America, and uses; they are uniform only in their depictions of Native American people. Some of the dolls were lovingly made by family members for their children to enjoy and/or to be a learning device for their very personal life styles. Others were made as commercial ventures to sell to tourists, and some were advertising pieces themselves. Over time, many have lost their original significance and become interesting to present-day people for very different reasons. They are united here as representatives of the diverse cultures that inspired them, and because each of them has been cherished and preserved by their subsequent owners over several generations.

Value ranges are provided for some of the dolls when they were available to be some help to readers who are not familiar with the market. They are not exact, and the market is different in various areas. Condition is a critical factor, so only the report of similar types of dolls can be offered.

Skookum woman doll with a clothes brush body, 7-1/2" h. Navajo man doll, c.1930s or earlier, 6-1/4" h. Navajo woman doll with a tag reading "Navajo Doll Authentically dressed with Indian hand loomed shawl Made in USA," 7-1/2" h. Navajo man valued $25 to 40.

Navajo man doll with carved wooden face, 12" h. Skookum style woman doll with buckskin, 11-1/4" h.

☼ *Eastern Woodland Dolls* ☼

Dolls representing Eastern Woodlands Indians are often made with corn husks because corn was an abundant crop throughout the north eastern region of North America. These groups were influenced in their dress by European fashions and materials. Many groups embellished their cloth costumes with European glass beadwork, and so the dolls reflect this preference. Dolls from this region are not plentiful as they were primarily made for Indian children, not for trade or sale. The many Indian groups in this area were driven further west in the seventeenth, eighteeth and early nineteenth centuries by colonists and government practices. Existing woodlands dolls are very special.

The Iroquois lived most abundantly in the region of New York state. This Iroquois corn cob doll, with a woven mask, is shown dancing on a wood fungus, 9-1/2" h. *Courtesy of Crown & Eagle Antiques* Valued $250 to 295.

Seneca Indians were a branch of the Iroquois who lived primarily in western
New York state and northwestern Pennsylvania. This corn husk doll of a Seneca
woman is dressed with wool clothing including elaborate beadwork and wearing
leather beaded moccasins, 13" h. *Courtesy of Crown & Eagle Antiques.*

German bisque American Indian doll incised 6/0 on the back of the head. The 5-piece composition body has brown sleep eyes and original clothes. These dolls were not based on any real person or photograph, but were simply the German dollmaker's idea of what an Indian would look like. Note the fierce expression. This type of doll was popular from approximately 1890 to 1920, 10" high. *Courtesy of The Doll Museum, Newport, R.I.*

German bisque doll incised Germany on the back of the head. The doll is a standard mold with a dark tone painted bisque finish. The felt clothes are original, including the "feather" headdress. This type of doll was made in regional dress costumes depicting almost any country and were exported to be sold as souvenirs, 4" high. *Courtesy The Doll Museum, Newport, R. I.*

Seminole Dolls

People living since pre-historic times along the Atlantic coast of Georgia and northern Florida may have been referred to by the visiting Spanish explorers as *cimarron* meaning "wild." They may have been a vagrant branch of the Creek tribe, for another derivation of their name means, in their language, "one who has camped out from the regular towns." (John R, Swanton, *The Indian Tribes of North America*, p. 139) In colonial America, these people were known as Seminoles.

Following the Creek-American war of 1813 to 1814, a group of Seminoles clustered in present Alachula County, Florida, where they formed the nucleus of the Seminole Nation. After the last Seminole War with the Army of the United States, 1835 to 1842, most Seminoles were moved to Seminole County, Oklahoma, at the western part of the Creek Nation.

Newcomers to the remaining group in Florida since the ninteenth century have included Muskogee Indians, and today the Seminole language is almost pure Muskogee.

Since the early twentieth century, Seminole Indians in northern Florida have made dolls dressed in lively cloth costumes which they sell at roadside stalls. Some are constructed with local cypress bark and roots in a variety of clothing styles. The black fabric on the head depicts the woven hairstyles traditionally worn by the tribal women and not a brimmed hat as is often assumed.

Values of old Seminole dolls today usually range between $45 and 200, depending on age, condition, and the type of market.

The remains of a Seminole woman doll, but look at the sewn-on label reading, "Florida Injun Doll, US Pat. 6-7-1932."

Old Seminole woman doll,
12-1/2" h.

Seminole man doll of considerable age with feet, arms of twisted bark, neckerchief, nose, and head wrapped in black fabric, 11" h. Value range $1500 and more for such a special doll.

Two Seminole women dolls, 6" h., with black hair.

Tall rag doll in Seminole woman's clothing, 13" h.

Single Seminole woman doll with yarn hair, 7" h.

Seminole woman doll
with a cedar bark face
and wearing a red
bead, multi-strand
necklace, 10" h.

Seminole woman
doll, 8" high.
*Courtesy of The
Doll Museum,
Newport, R.I.*

Four Seminole women dolls, c. 1930s, 4" h. to 9" h.

Group of seven Seminole women dolls, 3-3/4" h. to 10" h.

Top: Group of Seminole women dolls, 7" h., including an older one in front and a pincushion.
Value ranges for older one $45 to 55, pincushion $60 to 70, and others $30 to 40 each.

Group of three Seminole women dolls, 4-1/2" to 5-1/2" h.

Seminole woman doll with cypress root clothing, 12" h.

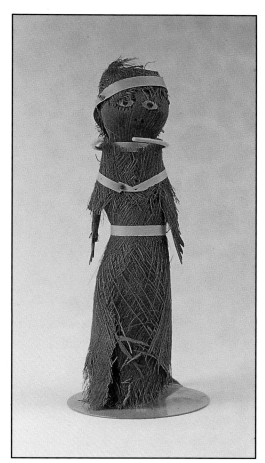

Seminole woman doll
without cloth clothes,
painted face, 7-1/2" h.

Three Seminole women dolls. *Courtesy of Crown & Eagle Antiques*
Value ranges from left, $20 to 25, $25 to 30, and $25 to 30.

Two Seminole women dolls, an older one and a newer one, 8-1/2" h. *Courtesy of Crown & Eagle Antiques* Value range for newer one $40 to 50.

Small Seminole girl doll, 3" h.

Next Page: Seminole woman doll, a fairly early one, 7-1/2" h.

Group of six Seminole women dolls, 4" to 5-1/2" h.

Seminole woman doll, 7-1/4" h.,
black head fabric with sequins.

Seminole woman doll, 7-1/4" h.,
black head fabric undecorated.

Group of five fairly modern Seminole woman dolls; three with
head fabric, one with yarn hair, one with tassel hair, 5" h. to 8" h.

Two Seminole
woman dolls with
black head fabric,
6-1/4" h. and 7" h.

Two Seminole
woman dolls with
black hair, 10" h.

Seminole woman doll
with faded brown fabric
clothing, 10" h.

Two rag dolls with Seminole
clothing, both with hands and
short legs of stuffed cloth, 10" h.

Celluloid manufactured
doll dressed in Seminole
clothing, 8" h.

Tall Seminole woman doll, 12" h., with tiny
doll dressed in Seminole clothing, 3" h.

Three Seminole women dolls, one with brown head fabric, 12-3/4" h.

Seminole basket with separate lid and a doll head finial, 4-1/2" d., 5-1/2" h., and pincushion with a Seminole doll head, 4" d., 5-1/4" h.

Seminole man doll, c.1920s, with a blue neckerchief, 10-3/4" h.;
and a Seminole woman doll, c. 1920s, 9-3/4" h.

Two Seminole women dolls, 5" h., yarn hair.

Three Seminole dolls: a woman doll with a spangle decorated hat and a tiny doll pinned to her clothing, 9-1/2" h.; tall Seminole woman doll, 16" h.; and a woman doll with plain black head fabric, 9" h.

☼ *Plains Dolls* ☼

The vast grasslands of the interior of North America provided endless roaming space for many Indian groups until the beginning of the nineteenth century. Nomadic in their lifestyles, they lived in the summers in portable teepees and carried infants on their backs in cradleboards. Dolls representing these people reflect this lifestyle and are lively, often dressed in buckskin clothing ornamented with colorful glass beads.

Photograph of two children, "Two Little Braves -Sac & Fox-," c. 1898, by F.A. Rinehart, Omaha, 8" x 6".

"Open Country" photograph by Carl Moon of Pasadena, California, c. 1904-1920, approximately 11" x 17."

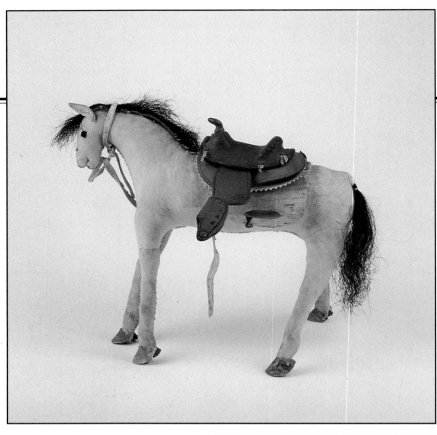

Plains pack horse with four parflesch, 8" h., Pack horse with leather salesman's sample saddle.

Plains man doll with beaded buckskin clothing, 12" h.

Plains painted teepee, 15" h., with
two small Skookum papoose dolls.

Back of a Plains painted teepee and two postcard
papoose dolls which went through the mail, 4" l.

Plains boy doll in buckskin pants and shirt with beadwork, 6" h. *Courtesy of Crown & Eagle Antiques*

Toy teepee with painted decoration and a plastic baby doll peeking out of the open flap, 8 1/4" h. *Courtesy of Crown & Eagle Antiques*

Sunlight and Shadow.—

Plains horsewoman doll with a papoose and beaded decoration, all covered in buckskin, 11-1/2" h. (continued on next page)

Previous Page:
"Sunlight and Shadow," woman with a cradelboard, photograph by Carl Moon, Pasadena, California, c. 1904-1920, approximately 11" X 17".

Plains horsewoman doll continued.

Plains woman doll with a plastic body and plush fabric clothing with painted decoration, 8" h.
Courtesy of Crown & Eagle Antiques

Indian dolls sold as souvenirs all over the
United States. The smaller doll is hard plastic,
8" high. The larger doll is vinyl, 12" high. No
attempt at realism was made in costuming
these dolls; they are merely representational in
a stereotypical view. *Courtesy of The Doll
Museum, Newport, R. I.*

Large felt man doll in Plains style buckskin clothing and with a full head-dress of colored felt feathers, 22" h. *Courtesy of Crown & Eagle Antiques*

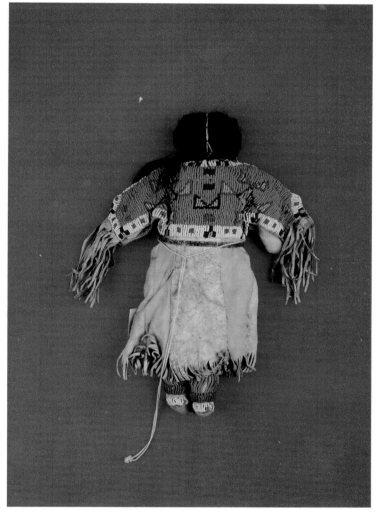

This is an unusual Sioux doll made for a young girl about 1900. The note accompanying it reads, "A little Indian girl's best doll, handmade by her grandmother out of skins. The bead work on it made it very special. The grandmother also used her own hair to make hair for the doll." 13 1/2" h.

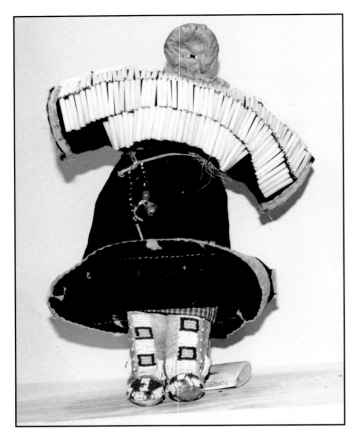

Old Sioux woman doll of leather with quillwork decoration on her black cloth dress and fine beaded boots. *Courtesy of Alaska on Madison, New York*

Four miniature cradle boards: from the top, Sioux beaded leather style; Cheyenne beaded leather with a stuffed baby doll; Sioux beaded style on a wooden frame with a Skookum baby perched inside; Apache laced board with a corn husk doll.

Eastern Sioux man doll with quillwork decoration on his jacket and beaded and shell earrings, a black wool shroud cloth, and human hair, c. 1870s.

The great Sioux group of the Dakota tribe was living in the general area now known as Wisconsin, Minnesota, and Iowa. The Sioux became adept paticularly at decorating their clothing with horizontal bands of colored glass beads across the chest. This woman tourist doll has Sioux beadwork on her dress and moccasins, 14 1/2" h. *Courtesy of Crown & Eagle Antiques*

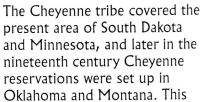
The Cheyenne tribe covered the present area of South Dakota and Minnesota, and later in the nineteenth century Cheyenne reservations were set up in Oklahoma and Montana. This Cheyenne woman doll has wonderful bead work on her deer hide dress and moccasins. She is ornamented with long hair braids and three strings of copper neck beads; she wears a quill breastplate and a leather belt with silver conchos, c. 1890, 18" h.

Cheyenne woman doll in hide clothing
with beadwork and human hair, c. 1875.

Cheyenne "Chief Thunderbird," photograph by Carl Moon, Pasadena, California, c. 1904-1920, 5 1/8" X 4 1/8".

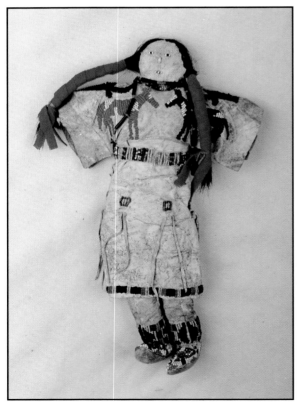 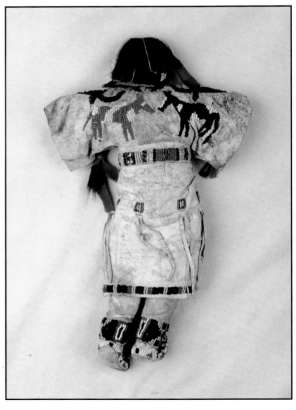

Fine Cheyenne woman doll made particularly interesting by the pictorial horses beaded on her dress, a highly unusual feature. *Courtesy of Lynn D. Trusdell*

Cheyenne man doll in buckskin clothing with painted decoration, labeled "Arapaho near Canadian River, Ok.," 12" h. *Courtesy of Crown & Eagle Antiques*

Cheyenne woman doll with beaded leather dress and human hair.

Below:
A pair of modern vinyl dolls produced by Sandy Dolls of Springfield, Mo. These 12" high dolls have somewhat ethnically correct facial features and carefully re-searched costume designs. They are sold as collectible playthings and currently retail about $36. *Courtesy of The Doll Museum, Newport, R. I.*

The Kiowa Apaches lived in the Southern Plains around the lands now known as Kansas. This pair of Kiowa Apache dolls of a man and a woman are dressed in deer hide clothing with beaded decoration, c. 1910, 14" h.

Two pottery storyteller dolls, a man and a woman with children made by Marie Suina, Cochiti Pueblo, New Mexico, c. 1980, 6 1/2" h. Private collection.

Pueblo Dolls

Along the Rio Grande in New Mexico are the homelands of tribes who live in mud brick pueblos, as they have for centuries. Potters at several of the pueblos skillfully have made dolls from clay. In the early 1960s, Helen Cordero of Cochiti Pueblo made a storyteller doll of her grandfather with many children climbing around him to listen to his stories. This theme has become popular and variations are often amusing.

Previous pages:
A pueblo with people and horses at the right, photograph by Carl Moon, Pasadena California, c. 1904-1920, approximately 11" X 17."

Woman with a pot on her head, photograph by Carl Moon,
Pasadena, California, c. 1904-1920, approximately 8" X 10."

Zuni Indians live in southwestern New Mexico where they are particularly
adept at making pottery and jewelry. This beaded woman doll, possibly Zuni
or Sioux, with a pot on her head, is wearing a cape, an apron, and a necklace, all made of small bead work, 6" h. *Courtesy of Crown & Eagle Antiques*

Hopi Dolls

The Hopi Indians, whose reservation is in northern Arizona, make flat wooden dolls as cradle toys to begin teaching their children the rich symbolism of colors and images in their culture. They also make cottonwood root replicas of their many gods known as Kachinas, for use in their homes and to sell to visitors; but Kachinas are not dolls in the sense of playings, and therefore are not a part of this study. Kachinas are represented in Hopi dances by carefully dressed men who take on the gods' attributes as they dance. They are fascinating and deeply traditional in their significance, making them a worthwhile interest to many people.

Two flat, wooden Hopi cradle toys painted with symbols
of the Hopi culture, 3 1/2" h. Private collection.

Dance group, photograph by Carl Moon, Pasadena, California, c. 1904-1920, approximately 11" X 17."

Hopi man dancer doll with a blue denim head sack and a
white body, 10-3/4" h. *Courtesy of Crown & Eagle Antiques*

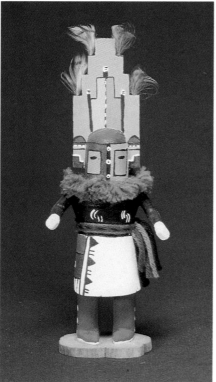

Top:
Cloth and buckskin woman doll with beading above the fringe, 13" h. The Hopi rag young woman doll with hair whorls has a traditional black dress and a cotton blanket shawl, 11-1/2" h. *Courtesy of Crown & Eagle Antiques*

Left:
Hopi Kachina doll of painted wood, c. 1983. Courtesy of The Doll Museum, Newport, R. I.

Navajo Dolls

The largest Indian reservation in the United States is that of the Navajo in northern Arizona. Navajo dolls depict the native people in their traditional occupations (as weavers, jewelry makers, and farmers) and in their traditional dress, which was inspired by Spanish explorers who had influence in these lands before the eighteenth century. The dolls have been a constant trade item for the Navajo since early in the twentieth century. Values of old Navajo dolls, approximately 8" h., made for sale to tourists, range $25 to 35 each on today's market.

Leather doll of a Navajo dancer with a beaded vest and a loin cloth, resting on a wooden base, 7-1/2" h. *Courtesy of Crown & Eagle Antiques*

Doll of a Navajo man dressed in beaded buckskin moccasins, shirt, trousers, and head piece with yarn hair, 11-1/2" h. Value range $250 to 300.

A buckskin doll of a Navajo man with horsehair hair and elaborate bead work, 8-1/2" h. A leather doll in two-color buckskin clothing and bead work around the face, 7" h. *Courtesy of Crown & Eagle Antiques*

Navajo man doll made of stuffed fabric with an embroidered face, buckskin shirt with bead decoration, felt trousers with bead decoration, and leather moccasins, 22-1/2" h. A Navajo woman doll of stuffed fabric with a painted face, red velvet blouse, a full cloth skirt, metal blouse decorations and concho belt, and a turquoise bead necklace, holding a papoose in a cradle board, 17" h. *Courtesy of Crown & Eagle Antiques*

Young girl with belt and necklaces, photograph by Carl Moon,
Pasadena, California, c. 1904-1920, approximately 8" X 10" h.

Navajo rag doll with yarn hair, a blue velvet shirt, concho belt, red skirt, and red moccasins, 18" h.

Left:
Navajo man doll with a red velvet shirt and white trousers, 11" h. *Courtesy of Crown & Eagle Antiques*

Bottom:
Pair of small Navajo woman dolls with fabric faces, beaded necklaces, and concho belts, 3-1/2" h. *Courtesy of Crown & Eagle Antiques*

Three children by a stone wall, photograph by Carl Moon,
Pasadena, California, c. 1904-1920, approximately 8" X 10" h.

Cloth Navajo woman doll with an embroidered face and a black shawl, 11-1/2" h. *Courtesy of Crown & Eagle Antiques*

Navajo man doll with a red velvet shirt and white pants, 11" h. *Courtesy of Crown & Eagle Antiques*

COPYRIGHT 1908 BY FRED HARVEY

Woman and child, both weaving, photograph
© 1908 by Fred Harvey, Albuquerque, New
Mexico, approximately 8" X 10" w.

Navajo woman doll at an upright
loom with a rug strung, 8" h. x 7" w.

Pair of Navajo dolls with ink painted faces in cloth heads, both with silver concho belts, 11-1/2" h. *Courtesy of Crown & Eagle Antiques* Value range $55 to 65 each.

Navajo weaving group with a pictorial rug on the loom and rag dolls of a man and woman. Frame 16" w x 14-3/4" h.

Three Navajo dolls, one man and two women, 7" h. *Courtesy of Crown & Eagle Antiques* Value range $25 to 30 each.

An upright loom with a Navajo woman doll shown weaving a rug with a papoose in a cradle board and a ball of wool, 11"w x 14" d. *Courtesy of Crown & Eagle Antiques*

Pair of Navajo stuffed dolls, a man and a woman in blue shirts, 7-3/4" h. *Courtesy of Crown & Eagle Antiques*

Two Navajo women dolls with stuffed pin cushion skirts, both with red velvet dresses and beadwork, 7" h. and 8" h. *Courtesy of Crown & Eagle Antiques* Value range $35 to 40 and $45 to 50.

Navajo man and woman dolls with rag heads, he in a red velvet shirt and
white trousers, 13" h., and she in a red velvet blouse and yellow print skirt.
Courtesy of Crown & Eagle Antiques Value range $65 to 75 the pair.

"A Deserted Lodge"

Near Chimney Buttes in Navaho Country.

KARL MOON

"A Deserted Lodge" near Chimney Buttes in
Navajo Country, photograph by Carl Moon,
c. 1904-1920, approximately 8" X 10" h.

Navajo woman doll shown as a weaver with
a rug on an upright loom, 11" h. x 10" w.
Courtesy of Crown & Eagle Antiques

left:
Two Navajo women dolls in black velvet shirts and colorful skirts and with painted cloth faces, 9-1/2" h. and 10" h. *Courtesy of Crown & Eagle Antiques* Value range $35 to 45 each.

Bottom Left:
Navajo woman doll with wrapped leggings and a black dress and wool plaid shawl. *Courtesy of Crown & Eagle Antiques*

Bottom Right:
Single Navajo rag woman doll with velvet clothing, 4" h. *Courtesy of Crown & Eagle Antiques*

Navajo man and woman dolls, c. 1980. *Kline's Galleries*

Navajo man and woman dolls, c. 1980.
Kline's Galleries

Yarn doll with a tray of Navajo wares and turquoise
beads, cottonwood, and weaving. She is dressed in
a velvet blouse and fabric skirt with a concho belt,
8" h. *Courtesy of Crown & Eagle Antiques*

Navajo papoose on a cradle board, 3-3/4" l.
Courtesy of Crown & Eagle Antiques Value
range $50 to 60.

Navajo bride doll, 7-1/2" h. in landscape
setting. Value range $100 to 145.

Pima Dolls

Below:
The Pima tribe lives in the arrid Gila River area of southern Arizona. This Pima "L'il Luv" buffalo dancer doll is of handmade construction with a stone hatchet, white rabbit fur clothing, and glass beads, c. 1970, 10" h. *Kline's Galleries*

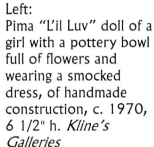

Left:
Pima "L'il Luv" doll of a girl with a pottery bowl full of flowers and wearing a smocked dress, of handmade construction, c. 1970, 6 1/2" h. *Kline's Galleries*

Pima "L'il Luv" woman doll holding a child, of handmade construction, c. 1970, 10" h. *Kline's Galleries*

Umatilla Dolls

The Umatilla tribe lives in the wet and mountainous area of the Umatilla and Columbia Rivers in Oregon. This Umatilla woman doll is of great rarity because it was made for an Indian child. The cradle board is made with a beaded strip of the sort found on blankets. The face is hide and the hair is human. This is one of the finest dolls known, c. 1870s.

Skookum Dolls

Skookum, the Bully Kiddo, 1916-17 © by Louis Amberg & Son under license from the Northwest Fruit Exchange, a national advertiser of Skookum apples. The doll resembles the fruit exchange's Indianhead trademark. The Exchange provided trade blankets for the region's Indian population in exchange for the local crop of apples. These dolls, made for sale to tourists in Oregon and Washington states, deptict no particular group of Indians (Native Americans), but represent the group in general. They usually are wrapped in a trade blanket and have no arms or hands. The bodies are stuffed, some with rectangular, fabric-covered bases. The earliest have apple faces, but since the apples did not hold up well, clay faces were used and still later, composition faces were used until about 1949. After about 1950, plastic faces and bodies appeared. Most Skookum dolls are shown looking to their right, or toward the rising sun, while a very few look left, to the setting sun.

Values for Skookum dolls vary widely today according to the age, condition, and type of market, most falling around $30 to 200 for an average 7-1/2" size.

Man and woman Skookum dolls in trade blankets, the man with a shell necklace, 11" h., and the woman with a bead necklace and a pappoose, 12-1/2" h.

Pair of Skookum dolls with tape moccasins. The man doll with turkey feathers, 17" h., and the woman doll with tapes braided in her hair, 16" h.

Two Skookum women dolls, one with a papoose and red moccasins, 13" h., the other
with a head kerchief, a papoose, and tape
moccasins, 12" h.

Two small Skookum dolls, an older one of a man
with a green head band and an orange paper
label, and a newer one with a larger head and
green moccasins. *Courtesy of Crown & Eagle
Antiques* Value range for the older one, $150
to 170 and for the newer one, $75 to 85.

Early apple face Skookum man
doll with black pants and
painted wooden feet, 12" h.

Pair of large Skookum men dolls, 22-1/2" h. and 24" h.,
each with leather moccasins and trade blankets.

Woman with blanket around her shoulders, photograph by Carl Moon, Pasadena, California, c. 1904-1920, 10" X 7 7/8".

Skookum pappoose labeled "Madame Hendren character doll, Costume Pat. May 9, 1916," doll 10" l. and the papoose bag 13" l.

Two Skookum-style wooden men dolls in trade blankets with painted feet, 10" h. and 11" h.

Skookum woman doll with eyes shifted left, instead of the usual right, 9-1/2" h.

Skookum doll with a painted face and glass eyes, a red head kerchief, and a trade blanket, 10" h.

Two Skookum dolls, a man, 11-1/2" h., and a woman with bead necklace, 10-1/2" h.

Two small girl Skookum dolls with painted leather moccasins, 6-1/4" h.

Seated Skookum style woman doll with black kerchief, 6" h.

Two Skookum women dolls, each with a papoose, the taller one with a bead and turquoise necklace, 12-1/2" h.; the shorter one with plastic moccasins marked "Trademark reg. Skookum bully good Indian Patented USA," 10-1/2" h.

Pair of Skookum women dolls with papooses. One is an older doll with a white head scarf and leather moccasins, 10-1/2" h. The other is a newer doll with a red head scarf and painted leather moccasins, 11" h. *Courtesy of Crown & Eagle Antiques*

Skookum baby doll in a blanket on a stuffed rectangular base, 4" h. *Courtesy of Crown & Eagle Antiques*

Skookum baby doll in a blanket on a stuffed rectangular base, 3 1/2" h. *Courtesy of Crown & Eagle Antiques*

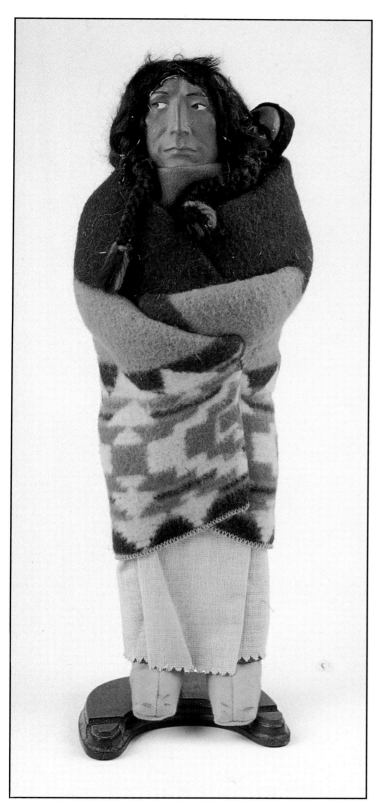

Skookum woman doll with a papoose, 14" h.
Courtesy of Crown & Eagle Antiques Value range
$295 to 325.

Tall Skookum man doll with a trade blanket, 15" h.

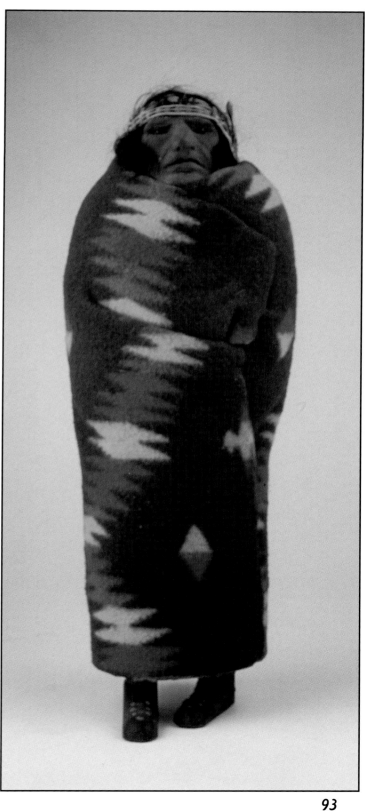

Large Skookum woman doll which was a store display figure, 35" h.

Large Skookum man doll which was a store display figure. He has fur shoes, leggings, a trade blanket, and wooden beads woven into his braided hair and as shirt buttons, 35" h.

Skookum woman doll with a stuffed papoose on a birch bark cradleboard, 6 3/4" h. *Courtesy of Crown & Eagle Antiques*

Skookum man doll with a peacepipe which is inscribed, "St. Labre Indian School," 12" l.

Skookum man doll in leather clothing with wooden beads stitched on and worn in two strands as necklaces, 35" h. *Courtesy of Crown & Eagle Antiques*

Three Skookum dolls, the largest 12" high.
Courtesy of The Doll Museum, Newport, R. I.

Skookum woman doll in leather clothing
with bead trim and a double row of beads
necklace, 35" h. *Courtesy of Crown &*
Eagle Antiques

Skookum woman doll in a cloth striped dress and a
short blanket wrap, bead necklace, paper moccasins.
A Skookum doll with red feathers in a head band, cloth
shirt and trousers, bead necklace, and a blanket wrap.

The Indians along the Pacific coast are fisher-men keenly aware of their severe climate. They balance the benefits of their water location with a backdrop of magnificent mountains. This Northwest bear doll has a wooden mask

and a basket pack, and is signed "Shona Hah,"
who is the maker Mary Smith and the matriarch
of the Lelooska Gallery in Ariel, Washington.
The mask tilts up to reveal a finely carved face,
c. 1980, 12-1/2" h. *Robin T. Mays Collection.*

Pair of Eskimo dolls. A man in a fur suit and boots with a wooden face, 9-1/2" h. A woman in a sealskin shammy dress and boots with a rag face and horsehair, 9" h. Value range $175 to 195 each.

Small Alaskan reindeer horn doll with carved face and fur parka, 6" h. *Courtesy of Crown & Eagle Antiques*

Three Eskimo dolls from Alaska, certified by the Alaska Native Arts & Crafts Clearing House (ANAC). Each has a reindeer horn body and a fur parka. They were made for and used as good luck charms for the first day of hunting. This type was made in the Kotzebue Sound region.

Eskimo doll with bone carved face wearing a fur parka and leggings, 8-1/2" h. *Courtesy of Crown & Eagle Antiques*

Eskimo man doll with carved wooden face in fur parka, leather mittens and boots, 9" h. *Courtesy of Crown & Eagle Antiques*

Eskimo man doll with rabbit skin parka, leather face, 10" h. *Courtesy of Crown & Eagle Antiques*

Alaskan tourist dolls of leather and fur, 20th century. The smaller doll has embroidered features, 9" high. The larger doll has ink drawn features, 10" high. *Courtesy of The Doll Museum, Newport, R. I.*

Eskimo man doll with carved wooden head, stuffed cloth with leather boots, denim pants, red parka, 20-1/2" h. *Courtesy of Crown & Eagle Antiques.*

Eskimo woman doll in white leather parka with white
rabbit trim, embroidered face, 16" h. *Courtesy of
Crown & Eagle Antiques*

Alaskan felt and leather doll with an illegible
ink mark on the bottom of a foot, probaby a
cottage industry product, with embroidered
features, 17" high. *Courtesy of The Doll
Museum, Newport, R. I.*

A gathering of contemporary dolls from the north country: back - Labradorian tea doll, Greenland doll, two Canadian Inuit women dolls, and a Canadian Inuit ghost doll; center - Alaskan doll in fur parka; front - two Canadian antler and skin dolls seated on a log. *Courtesy of Alaska on Madison, New York*

Alaskan ivory doll with fur parka and leather boots. *Courtesy of Alaska on Madison, New York.*

Called "The Uglies" by their makers, a mother-daughter team from Alaska, these contemporary leather-faced women dolls have lots of individual personality. *Courtesy of Alaska on Madison, New York.*

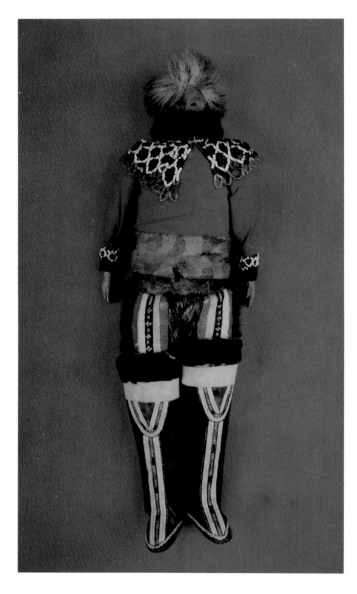

Greenland man doll with a wooden head and hands and stuffed legs, dressed in a red shirt and tall sealskin boots with quill decoration, c. 1900, 20" h. *Courtesy of Crown & Eagle Antiques*

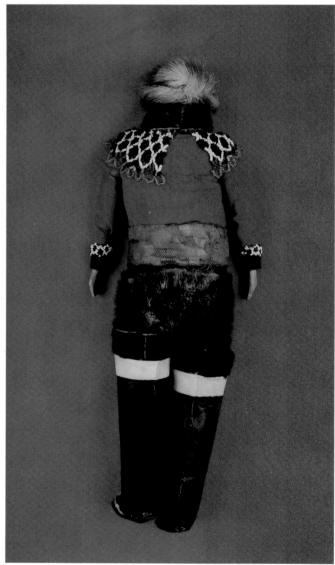

Shaman doll of ivory and a fur parka, c. 1880, from Point Hope, Alaska. *Courtesy of Alaska on Madison, New York City.*

☼ *Index* ☼